ROBO GAMI

MUNEJI FUCHIMOTO
CREATOR OF
ORIROBO™

**FOLD YOUR OWN ROBOTS
AND BATTLE YOUR FRIENDS**

English language rights, translation & production by
World Book Media LLC.
info@worldbookmedia.com

Translator: Kyoko Matthews
English Editor: Lindsay Fair
Technical Editor: Jason Ku
Design: Arati Devasher, www.aratidevasher.com

First English edition published in the United States of America in 2015 by
Quarry Books, a member of
Quarto Publishing Group USA Inc.
100 Cummings Center
Suite 406-L
Beverly, Massachusetts 01915-6101
www.quarrybooks.com
Visit www.craftside.net for a behind-the-scenes peek at our crafty world!

ISBN: 978-1-63159-052-8

Library of Congress Cataloging-in-Publication Data not available at time
of printing.

Printed in China

10 9 8 7 6 5 4 3 2 1

MUNEJI FUCHIMOTO is the president
and art director of graphic design firm
SCOG Design Inc. Inspired by a project
his son made in his kindergarten class,
Fuchimoto began creating original
origami designs in 2005. He is the
author of multiple origami books in
Japan and is known for his unique robot
and animal designs.

DATE: 2240.01.07
INTELLIGENCE REPORT:

THE STORY OF ROBOGAMI

Technological advancements lead to the development of Paper AI, a thin and strong material equipped with artificial intelligence. When Paper AI is folded, it possesses the ability to transform and assume the power of the finished shape.

One day, a batch of Paper AI is improperly disposed of and mutates into an evil robot known as SHRED. Scientists develop ROBOGAMI to protect humankind from SHRED.

The ROBOGAMI successfully defeat SHRED and save the Earth from destruction. Scientists produce WORKROBO to re-cultivate the Earth and repair the damage done by the war.

DATE: 2245.05.12 | REPORT:
The WORKROBO are unexpectedly attacked by legions of mysterious enemy robots. Intelligence report reveals the threat is a deadly new form of SHRED. WORKROBO lack capability to fight and are immediately destroyed.

WORKROBO WR02
PAGE 12

SHRED 310
PAGE 27

ORIROBO OR201
PAGE 20

PAGE 20

UPDATE:
ORIROBO OR201 is developed to fight against the new form of SHRED. During battle, SHRED copies the ORIROBOS' characteristics and mutates making defeat impossible. A new solution is imperative to destroy SHRED once and for all.

DATE: 2250.09.25 | REPORT:
Humans successfully produce three uncopiable fighters called ORISOLDIERS. Armed with individual weapons, the ORISOLDIERS are the most advanced ROBOGAMI ever created. These powerful soldiers fight against their enemies to protect the Earth. The mystery robots are destroyed completely and mankind wins the battle.

ORISOLDIER K562
PAGE 38

ORISOLDIER N534
PAGE 33

ORISOLDIER M497
PAGE 41

BASIC FOLDING TECHNIQUES

In order to make the designs included in this book, you'll need to master a few basic origami techniques.

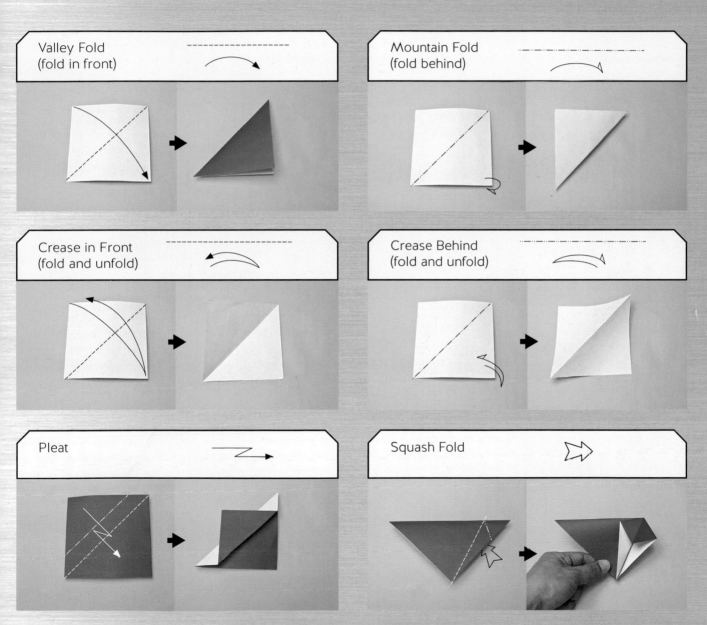

Valley Fold
(fold in front)

Mountain Fold
(fold behind)

Crease in Front
(fold and unfold)

Crease Behind
(fold and unfold)

Pleat

Squash Fold

SYMBOL LEGEND

You'll encounter the following symbols throughout the individual project instructions. These symbols represent actions commonly used in origami.

 Imaginary line

 View from the indicated direction

 Zoom in

 Rotate

 Pull out

 Zoom out

 Turn over

Push in

Crimp Inside

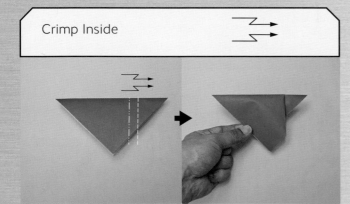

Crimp Outside

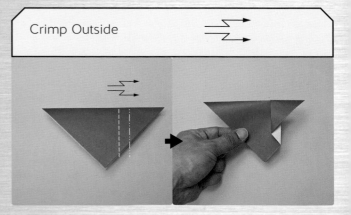

Inside Reverse Fold

Outside Reverse Fold

Rabbit Ear Fold

Crimp at an Angle
(make two inside reverse folds)

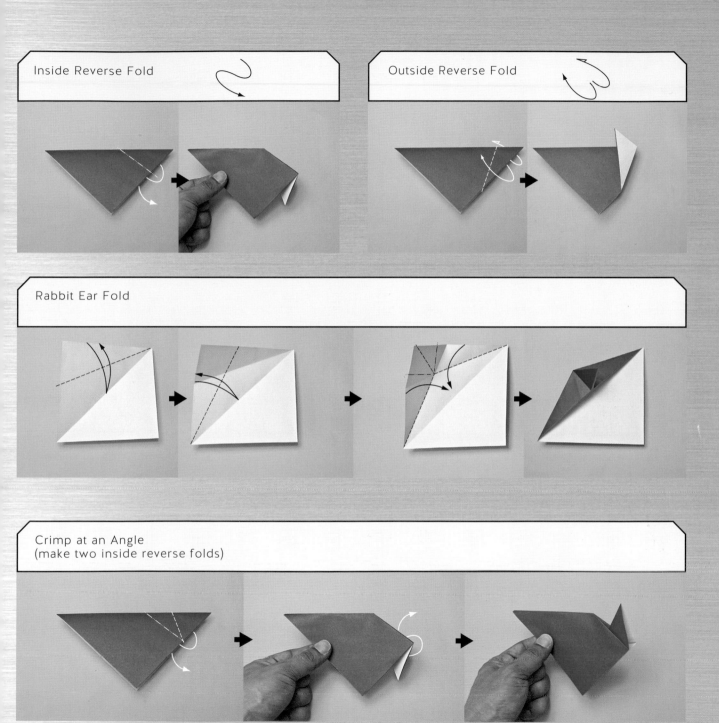

BASIC STARTING SHAPES FOR ROBOGAMI

Most of the ROBOGAMI designs start with one of these basic shapes. Master these folds to produce better finished models.

SHAPE A

1 Fold in half from edge to edge.

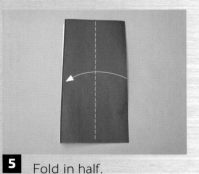

2 Fold the top layer in half.

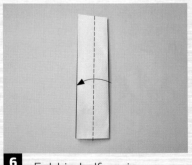

3 Fold the top layer in half again.

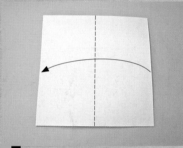

4 Crease firmly.

Turn over

5 Fold in half.

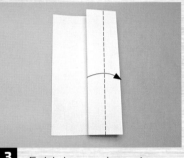

6 Fold in half again.

7 Unfold everything.

8 The vertical creases are complete.

Rotate 90°

9 Repeat steps 1–7.

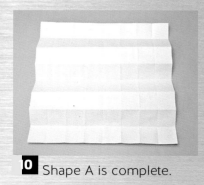

0 Shape A is complete.

SHAPE B

1 Follow steps 1–9 above to complete shape A.

2 Fold along the outermost creases while pinching the corners in half, flattening them up and down.

3 Shape B is complete.

WORKROBO
WR02

SHOWN ON PAGE 4

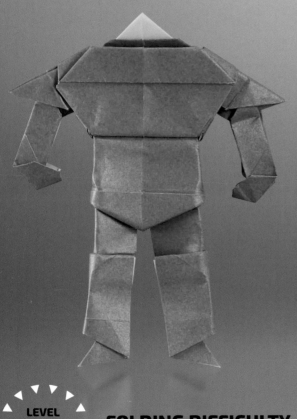

Known for its ability to regenerate, WORKROBO WR02 possesses strong healing powers.

LEVEL 11

FOLDING DIFFICULTY
★★★★★★★

MACHINE DATA

TYPE	WORKER
POWER	★
SPEED	★★
OFFENSIVE POWER	★★
DEFENSIVE POWER	★★★
FEATURES	» POSESSES ABILITY TO REGENERATE » USES LASER BEAM TO HEAL WOUNDS
ABILITY TO FLY	X

1 Make starting shape A, as shown on page 10.

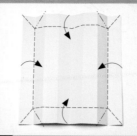

2 Fold along the outermost creases while pinching the corners in half, flattening them up and down.

3 Crease firmly. You have now completed starting shape B, as shown on page 11.

4 Fold in along the outermost creases while pinching the corners in half, flattening them up and down.

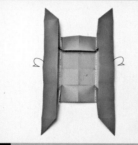

5 Fold the sides behind along existing creases.

6 Fold the edges into the center, opening the layers and squash folding.

7 Rabbit ear fold the section marked by the Δ. Refer to the sidebar for detailed instructions.

A. First, make the crease by folding the triangle in half and unfolding. Repeat for opposite side.

B. Fold both ends and raise the center.

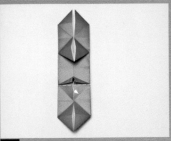

8 Fold the flap down, inserting the small center flap through the central slit.

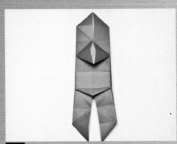

9 Completed view of step 8.

Zoom in

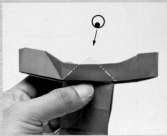

10 Open the top center edges only and squash fold up.

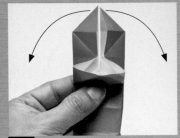

11 Pull the upper flaps to the sides. Do not flatten.

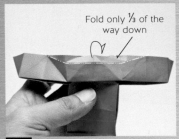

Fold only ⅓ of the way down

12 Mountain fold the top edge behind as shown.

13 Rewrap the paper around along existing creases.

View from the front.

View from the back. Close the flap back up.

14 Fold diagonally from point to point.

Note: It's alright if the paper rips slightly. The tears will not be visible on the finished project.

15 Fold to the right along the existing crease.

16 Crease firmly and unfold.

17 Open the layers on both sides.

18 Pinch crease A by pushing from the inside with your finger.

19 Pinch mountain folds along the creases shown.

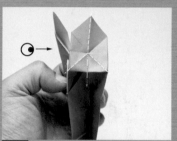

20 Push in the center and collapse along the creases shown.

Detailed view of step 20 in progress.

21 Repeats steps 14-20 for the left side.

22 Pleat in front as shown.

23 Completed view of step 22.

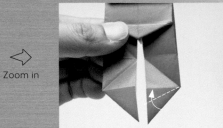

Zoom in

24 Fold diagonally from edge to crease as shown.

25 Fold the flap out diagonally.

26 Completed view of step 25.

27 Unfold, then crimp (inside reverse fold twice) along existing creases.

28 Pleat in front as shown.

29 Repeat steps 24-28 for the other leg. Fold toward inside using inside reverse fold.

30 Completed view of step 29.

Turn over

31 Fold the edge to the center while opening and squash folding the upper part.

32 Repeat step 31 on the other leg.

33 Completed view of step 32. Note: The circled section is magnified in the next step.

Zoom out

34 Inside reverse fold the corner as shown.

Zoom in

Side view of step 34.

35 Fold the other side in the same way.

Zoom out

Turn over

36 Pull the legs apart.

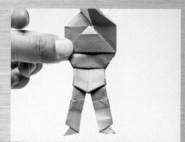

37 Completed view of step 36.

Turn over

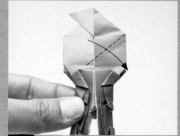

38 Fold the right flap down diagonally.

39 Completed view of step 38.

Zoom in

Turn over

40 Fold internal flap A over and tuck inside as shown.

Side view of the tucking process.

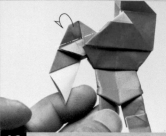

41 Fold the outer flap behind.

42 Fold the next section in the same way as step 40.

View from the bottom.

43 Fold the outer flap behind.

44 Outside reverse fold the tip of the hand.

45 Outside reverse fold to complete the hand.

46 Repeat steps 38-45 for the other arm.

47 Pleat behind as shown.

WORKROBO WR02 is complete!

ORIROBO
OR201

SHOWN ON PAGE 5

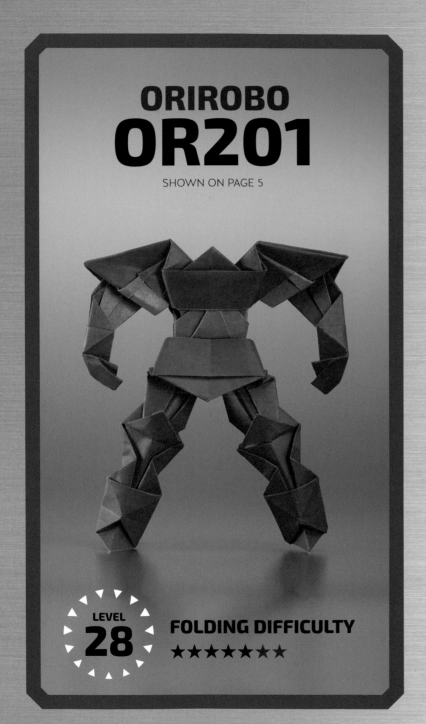

LEVEL
28

FOLDING DIFFICULTY

★★★★★★★

ORIROBO OR201 was developed based on the original SUPER ORIROBO that saved the Earth from danger long ago.

MACHINE DATA	
TYPE	FIGHTER
POWER	★★★★★
SPEED	★★★★★★
OFFENSIVE POWER	★★★★★★
DEFENSIVE POWER	★★★★★★
FEATURES	» MEGA SHOULDER ATTACK » MEGA KICK » MEGA CRUSH PUNCH
ABILITY TO FLY	X

1 Make starting shape B, as shown on page 11.

Turn over

2 Fold along the outermost creases while pinching the corners in half, flattening them up and down.

3 Completed view of step 2.

Zoom in

4 Pleat along the creases shown.

5 Crease firmly and unfold, opening out the layers.

6 Pinch mountain folds along the creases shown.

7 Collapse down along the existing creases as shown.

8 Repeat steps 4-7 on the three remaining corners.

Turn over

Rotate

9 Fold along the outermost creases while pinching the corners in half, standing them up.

21

10 Flatten the top two corners out to the left and right. Open and squash fold the bottom two corners.

11 Completed view of step 10. Note: The circled section is magnified in the next step.

Zoom in

Rotate

12 Fold edge to edge.

13 Fold the edge to the centerline and unfold.

14 Crease the left side in the same way.

15 Fold the flap up along existing creases.

In progress view. Bring the edges to the center to complete the petal fold.

16 Repeat steps 12–15 on the remaining bottom corner.

Rotate

17 Fold and unfold along the diagonals.

22

18 Lift the center point out while bringing the four corners together behind using existing creases.

Zoom in

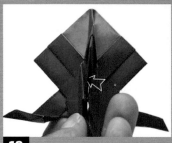

19 Open the layers and squash fold.

20 Inside reverse fold along the creases shown.

21 Inside reverse fold in the same way on the left.

22 Completed view of step 21.

Turn over

23 Open the layers and squash fold.

Mountain folds come to a point (this will be the head)

24 Inside reverse fold both sides symmetrically as shown.

25 Fold the edges to the center and unfold.

26 Fold the flaps up along existing creases.

27 Bring the edges to the center to complete the petal fold.

28 Completed view of step 27.

Turn over

29 Fold the corner up and tuck into the pocket shown.

30 Mountain fold the side flaps behind.

Zoom out

Turn over

A view from behind. The next step will focus on the head on the other side.

Zoom in

Turn over

Rotate

31 Pull the flaps to the sides. Do not flatten.

32 Crimp the head inside along the creases shown.

33 Flatten down and view from the front.

Rotate

34 Pull the right flap down with an inside reverse fold.

35 Fold up one layer along the crease shown while pulling out some internal paper.

36 Mountain fold a small corner behind. Fold the lower arm closed.

37 Pleat behind as shown.

38 Completed view of step 37.

Turn over

39 Pull the edge down and squash fold as shown.

40 Completed view of step 39.

Turn over

41 Pleat the front layer and squash fold as shown.

42 Crimp inside along the creases shown.

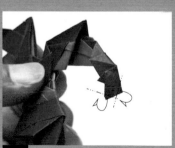

43 Shape the hand by mountain folding the small corners behind.

44 Repeat steps 34-43 for the left arm.

Zoom out

45 Open the left leg and view from below.

46 Pleat the upper layer of the leg and flatten the leg to the side.

47 Fold the knee corner up.

48 Crimp the foot with two inside reverse folds while mountain folding the leg in half.

49 Repeat steps 45–48 on the left leg.

ORIROBO OR201 is complete!

SHRED
SH310

SHOWN ON PAGE 4

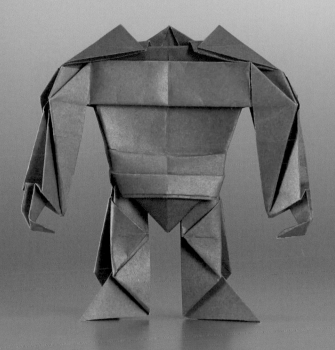

SHOWN ON PAGE 4

LEVEL
12

FOLDING DIFFICULTY
★★★★☆☆☆

SHRED SH310 is a mysterious robot who can destroy WORKROBO using his immense power.

MACHINE DATA	
TYPE	DESTROYER
POWER	★★★★
SPEED	★
OFFENSIVE POWER	★★★
DEFENSIVE POWER	★
FEATURES	» CRUSH PUNCH
ABILITY TO FLY	X

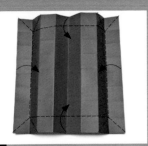

1 Make starting shape A, as shown on page 10. Fold along the outermost creases while pinching the corners in half, flattening them up and down.

2 Open and squash fold the top two corners.

Zoom in

3 Fold the edges to the centerline and unfold.

4 Fold the corner up and bring the edges to the center. This is known as the petal fold.

5 Completed view of step 4. Repeat steps 3-4 on the top right corner.

Zoom out

6 Fold the top and bottom edges behind and fold the bottom corners outward.

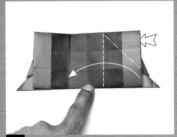

7 Open the layers and squash fold as shown.

8 Pleat the front layer as shown and squash fold.

9 Fold the top layer to the right.

10 Fold the edge to the centerline and unfold.

11 Repeat step 10 on the right. Fold the bottom flaps forward.

12 Fold the flap up and bring the edges to the center to complete the petal fold.

13 Fold the flap back down.

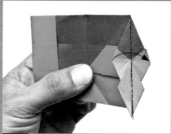

14 Fold the flap in half as shown.

15 Pleat the top layer and rotate the left corner down as shown.

16 Pleat the bottom flap diagonally as shown.

17 Unfold.

18 Open the layers on both sides.

19 Pinch mountain and valley folds along the creases shown.

In progress view. Collapse flat.

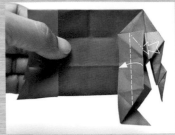

20 Fold edge to edge while squash folding the upper part.

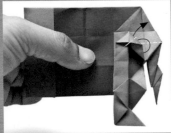

21 Inside reverse fold as shown.

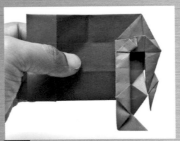

22 Repeat steps 7–21 on the left side.

Turn over

23 Valley fold up.

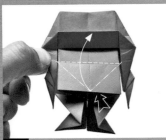

24 Fold up and bring the edges to the center to complete the petal fold.

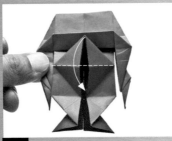

25 Fold the corner down.

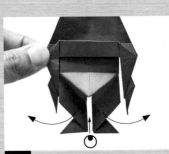

26 Open the legs apart. Do not flatten.

27 Fold edge to edge and unfold.

28 Fold up one layer.

29 Fold down two layers. Make sure to offset the two layers as shown in step 30.

30 Pleat the right leg back into position as shown.

In progress view.

31 Collapse down the left leg in the same way.

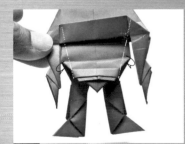

32 Mountain fold the sides behind through all layers to thin the body.

▷
Zoom out

33 Fold diagonally as shown.

34 Crease firmly.

35 Valley fold down the inner layer only.

36 Valley fold the inner corner back up forming a pleat.

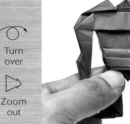

37 Rotate the end of the arm by pulling out some inner layers.

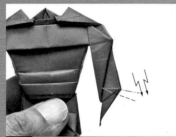

38 Crimp inside by rotating the end of the arm.

39 Outside reverse fold the tip to form a claw.

40 Repeat steps 37–39 on the left side.

SHRED SH310 is complete!

ORISOLDIER N534

SHOWN ON PAGE 6

SHOWN ON PAGE 6

As the leader of all the soldiers, ORISOLDIER N534 has excellent fighting ability and high attack capability.

MACHINE DATA

TYPE	SOLDIER
POWER	★★★★★★ (★)
SPEED	★★★★★★ (★)
OFFENSIVE POWER	★★★★★★ (★)
DEFENSIVE POWER	★★★★★★ (★)
FEATURES	» GALAXY ATTACK » CYCLONE ATTACK
ABILITY TO FLY	X

(★) INDICATES ADDITIONAL STRENGTH WHEN EQUIPPED WITH POWER UP ITEMS

POWER UP ITEMS

ORISOLDIER N534

Cosmo Radar Wing

Cosmo Power Guard

Power Sword

LEVEL
31

FOLDING DIFFICULTY

★★★★☆☆☆

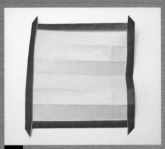

1 Make starting shape B, as shown on page 11.

Turn over

2 Fold in along the inner 4 x 4 square while pinching the corners in half, flattening the top corners to the sides and the bottom corners down.

3 Pleat the bottom right flap diagonally as shown. Note: The circled section is magnified in the next step.

Zoom in

4 Crease firmly and unfold.

5 Open the layers on both sides.

6 Pinch mountain and valley folds along the creases shown.

In progress view. Collapse flat.

7 Pull open one layer from behind. Do not flatten.

8 Pleat through all layers making the valley fold along the existing crease.

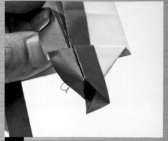

9 Fold back the layer pulled out in step 7.

Zoom out

10 Repeat steps 3–9 on the left.

Zoom out

11 Pleat as shown, but only fold halfway. Do not flatten.

12 Completed view of step 11.

Turn over

13 Fold the center of the bottom edge to the crease shown, folding to the corners on the sides.

14 Finish collapsing the pleats from step 11 down flat.

15 Completed view of step 14.

Zoom in

Turn over

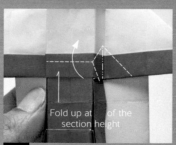

Fold up at   of the section height

16 Reopen the central pleats and fold the center edge up along the creases shown.

In progress view. Collapse in the same way on both sides.

Zoom out

17 Pleat along the creases shown but only halfway. Do not flatten.

18 Inside reverse fold the side edges in as shown while collapsing flat the pleat from step 17.

19 Valley fold the side edges in and tuck them into the body.

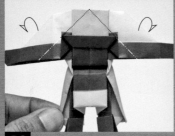

20 Mountain fold the side flaps down as shown.

21 Completed view of step 20.

Zoom in

Turn over

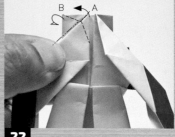

22 Fold flap B behind while outside reverse folding corner A to the side.

In progress view. Collapse flat.

Turn over

23 Fold the corner inward underneath other layers.

24 Repeat steps 22–23 on the left.

25 Inside reverse fold by pulling out the edges shown.

26 Pleat the edges shown and squash fold underneath other layers.

27 Pleat the right flap diagonally as shown.

Zoom in

28 Shape the hand by mountain folding the small corners behind.

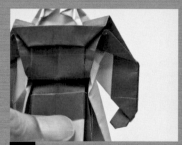

29 Repeat steps 27–28 for the left arm.

Zoom out

ORISOLDIER N534 is complete!

ORISOLDIER
K562

SHOWN ON PAGE 6

As a master of spearfighting, ORISOLDIER K562 is the No.1 ranked fighter among the soldiers. He is especially skilled at high speed combat.

MACHINE DATA

TYPE	SOLDIER
POWER	★★★★★ (★)
SPEED	★★★★★★★
OFFENSIVE POWER	★★★★★★ (★)
DEFENSIVE POWER	★★★★★ (★)
FEATURES	» SPEAR FLUSH » THUNDER SPEAR
ABILITY TO FLY	X

(★) INDICATES ADDITIONAL STRENGTH WHEN EQUIPPED WITH POWER UP ITEMS

POWER UP ITEMS

ORISOLDIER K562

Cosmo Radar Wing

Cosmo Power Guard

Power Spear

LEVEL 31

FOLDING DIFFICULTY
★★★★★★★

1 Complete steps 1-15 of ORISOLDIER N534 on pages 34-35. Open the central pleats.

Zoom in

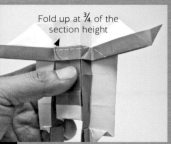

Fold up at ¾ of the section height

2 Fold the center edge up along the creases shown.

In progress view. Collapse the right side flat.

3 Collapse the left side in the same way.

4 Look at the model from the right.

Zoom in

5 Fold edge to edge while inside reverse folding.

6 Inside reverse fold the arm down as shown.

7 Repeat steps 5-6 for the left arm.

Zoom out

8 Pleat along the creases shown, but only halfway. Do not flatten.

9 Inside reverse fold the side edges in as shown, while collapsing flat the pleat from step 8.

10 Valley fold the side edges in and tuck them into the body.

11 Valley fold the corners to the center.

12 Fold the corners inward underneath other layers. Use tweezers if necessary.

13 Follow steps 27-29 of ORISOLDIER N534 on page 37 to fold the hands.

ORISOLDIER K562 is complete!

ORISOLDIER
M497

SHOWN ON PAGE 6

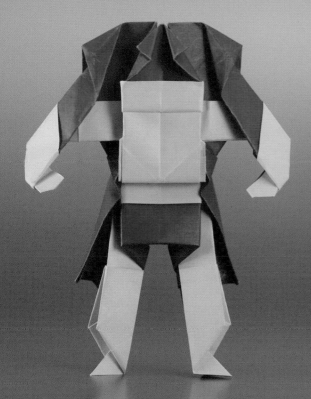

LEVEL
30

FOLDING DIFFICULTY
★★★★★★★

ORISOLDIER M497 is a hunter who skillfully attacks enemies using a laser arrow sword.

MACHINE DATA

TYPE	SOLDIER
POWER	★★★★★(★)
SPEED	★★★★★★★
OFFENSIVE POWER	★★★★★(★)
DEFENSIVE POWER	★★★★★★(★)
FEATURES	» LASER ARROW ATTACK » ARROW SWORD SMASH
ABILITY TO FLY	X

(★) INDICATES ADDITIONAL STRENGTH WHEN EQUIPPED WITH POWER UP ITEMS

POWER UP ITEMS

ORISOLDIER M497

Cosmo Radar Wing

Cosmo Power Guard

Laser Arrow Sword

 **1** Complete steps 1-3 of ORISOLDIER K562 on page 39. Fold the corner in diagonally.

 **2** Fold the corner back to the right using a vertical crease.

 **3** Valley fold the arm down diagonally.

 **4** Open the bottom layers and flatten down, as with a squash fold.

 **5** Repeat steps 1–4 on the left side.

 **6** Follow steps 8-10 and 13 on pages 39-40 to finish the body and hands in the same way as ORISOLDER K562.

 ORISOLDIER M497 is complete!

COSMO
RADAR
WING

SHOWN ON PAGE 33

FOLDING DIFFICULTY

★★☆☆☆☆☆

NOTE: FOR THIS MODEL, USE A SHEET
OF PAPER THAT IS ¼ OF THE SIZE
USED FOR THE SOLDIERS.

1 Fold in half diagonally.

2 Rabbit ear fold the flap.
Start by folding edge to edge
and unfolding as shown.

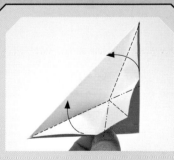

Bring the edges of the
triangle together, collapsing
along the creases shown.

3 Open the layers and and squash fold.

4 Fold the edges to the center and unfold.

5 Fold the point down and bring the edges to the center to complete the petal fold.

6 Completed view of step 5.

Turn over

7 Rabbit ear fold by repeating steps 1-2 on page 43.

8 Open the center flap and squash fold.

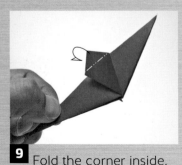

9 Fold the corner inside.

10 Fold the corners behind.

11 Inside reverse fold the flaps diagonally.

2 Completed view of step 11.

Turn over

13 Fold the central layers together while inside reverse folding corner A forward.

COSMO RADAR WING is complete!

HOW TO EQUIP A SOLDIER WITH A COSMO RADAR WING

1 Turn the soldier over so you can insert the wing into his back.

2 Fold the soldier in half a little and slide the flaps into the center pockets.

3 After inserting, flatten the soldier back out.

ORISOLDIER N534 is now equipped with a COSMO RADAR WING!

COSMO POWER GUARD

SHOWN ON PAGE 6

FOLDING DIFFICULTY

★★☆☆☆☆☆

NOTE: FOR THIS MODEL, USE A SHEET OF PAPER THAT IS ¼ OF THE SIZE USED FOR THE SOLDIERS.

1 Mountain fold diagonally and unfold.

2 Fold two opposite corners to the center.

3 Mountain fold the edges into the center.

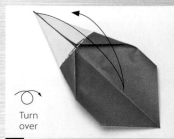

4 Valley fold as shown and unfold.

Turn over

5 Fold corner A down while opening out the side layers as shown.

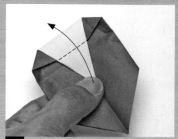

6 Fold the corner back as shown.

7 Repeat steps 3–5 on the other corner.

8 Completed view of step 7.

Turn over

COSMO POWER GUARD is complete!

HOW TO EQUIP A SOLDIER WITH A COSMO POWER GUARD

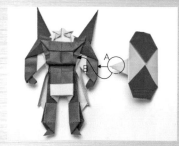

Insert the circled section of the flap into either pocket A or B.

COSMO POWER GUARD inserted into pocket A of ORISOLDIER N534.

COSMO POWER GUARD inserted into pocket B of ORISOLDIER N534.

POWER SWORD

SHOWN ON PAGE 6

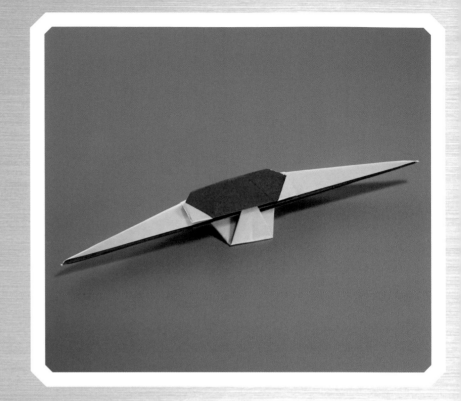

FOLDING DIFFICULTY

★★☆☆☆☆☆

NOTE: FOR THIS MODEL, USE A SHEET
OF PAPER THAT IS ¼ OF THE SIZE
USED FOR THE SOLDIERS.

1 Mountain fold
diagonally and unfold.

2 Fold the edges to the
center and unfold.

3 Repeat step 2 on the
other three corners.

4 Crease valley fold lines connecting the crease intersections shown.

5 Mountain fold the bottom right corner behind.

6 Collapse along the creases shown.

  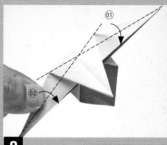

Turn over

7 Completed view of step 6.

8 Collapse along the creases shown.

9 Thin each flap in half by folding edge to edge (first flap ①, then flap ②).

Zoom out

Turn over

Zoom in

10 Crease firmly.

11 Valley fold in-line with the edge behind.

12 Valley fold the corner underneath the layers shown.

13 Completed view of step 12.

Turn over

14 Valley fold the corner, wrapping around the other layers.

15 Mountain fold the corner inside.

16 Completed view of step 15.

Turn over

Zoom out

POWER SWORD is complete!

HOW TO EQUIP A SOLDIER WITH A POWER SWORD

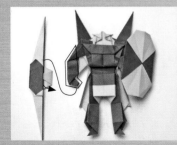

Insert the arm inside the sword layers.

In progress view. Slide the arm all the way in.

ORISOLDIER N534 is now equipped with a POWER SWORD.

POWER SPEAR

SHOWN ON PAGE 6

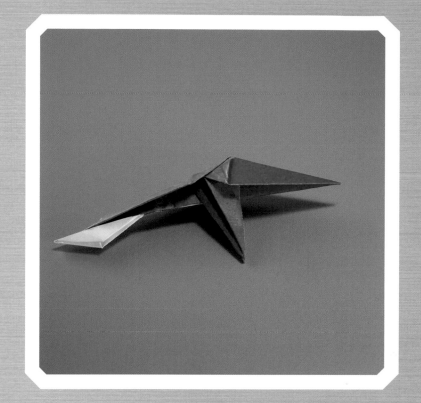

FOLDING DIFFICULTY

★★★★★★★

NOTE: FOR THIS MODEL, USE A SHEET OF PAPER THAT IS ¼ OF THE SIZE USED FOR THE SOLDIERS.

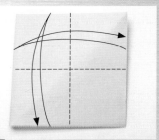

1 Fold edge to edge and unfold.

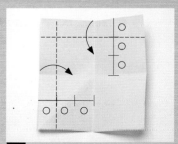

2 Fold in two neighboring edges ⅓ of the way to the center.

3 Crease firmly and unfold.

4 Fold the corners in to the creases.

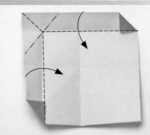

5 Fold the edges back in while folding the corner in half and to the side.

6 Fold edge to crease and unfold.

Zoom in

Rotate

7 Outside reverse fold the corner along existing creases.

Zoom out

8 Open the layers and flatten as with a squash fold.

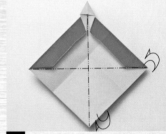

9 Mountain fold along the diagonals.

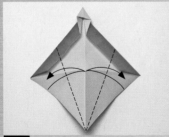

10 Fold the edges to the center and unfold.

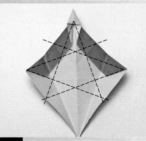

11 Repeat step 10 on the other three corners.

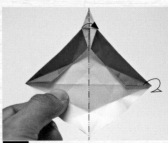

12 Mountain fold in half while valley folding the upper part closed.

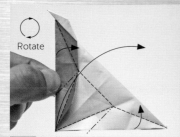

Rotate

13 Collapse along the creases shown.

14 Repeat step 13 behind.

Turn over

15 Completed view of step 14. Reorient the model.

Rotate

Turn over

16 Inside reverse fold as shown.

17 Crimp outside by pleating each side down as shown.

18 Valley fold one layer diagonally as shown.

19 Repeat step 18 behind.

HOW TO EQUIP A SOLDIER WITH A POWER SPEAR

POWER SPEAR is complete!

Insert into the gap in the elbow.

ORISOLDIER K562 is now equipped with a POWER SPEAR.

LASER ARROW SWORD

SHOWN ON PAGE 6

FOLDING DIFFICULTY

★★★★★★★

NOTE: FOR THIS MODEL, USE A SHEET
OF PAPER THAT IS ¼ OF THE SIZE
USED FOR THE SOLDIERS.

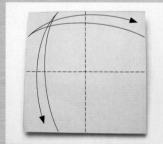

1 Fold edge to edge
and unfold.

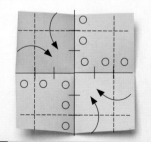

2 Fold each edge in ⅓ of
the way to the center.

3 Crease firmly and unfold.

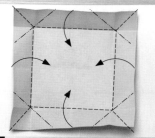

4 Fold the edges in, folding each corner in half, flattening the top corners up, and the bottom corners to the sides.

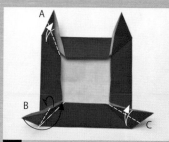

5 Fold edge to crease at A and C and unfold. Valley fold corner B in as shown.

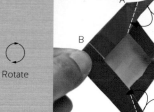

6 Outside reverse fold corners A and C along existing creases.

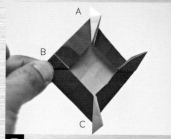

7 Completed view of step 6. Focus on corner A.

Zoom in

8 Open the layers and flatten as with a squash fold. Repeat on corner C.

Zoom out

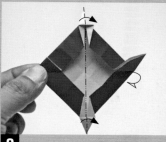

9 Mountain fold in half while valley folding the upper and lower parts closed.

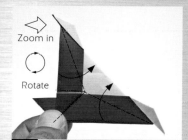

Zoom in

Rotate

10 Rabbit ear fold by bringing the edges together as shown.

11 Completed view of step 10.

Turn over

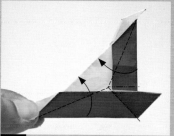

12 Repeat step 10 on this side.

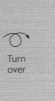

Turn over

13 Completed view of step 12.

14 Valley fold the corner into the pocket on the other side.

LASER ARROW SWORD is complete!

HOW TO EQUIP A SOLDIER WITH A LASER ARROW SWORD

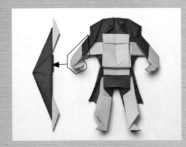

Zoom in

Zoom out

Insert the arm into the gap.

In progress view. Insert the arm into the pocket in the back.

ORISOLDIER M497 is now equipped with a LASER ARROW SWORD.

DID YOU THINK THE STORY WAS OVER? MEET THE SPACE SCORPION...

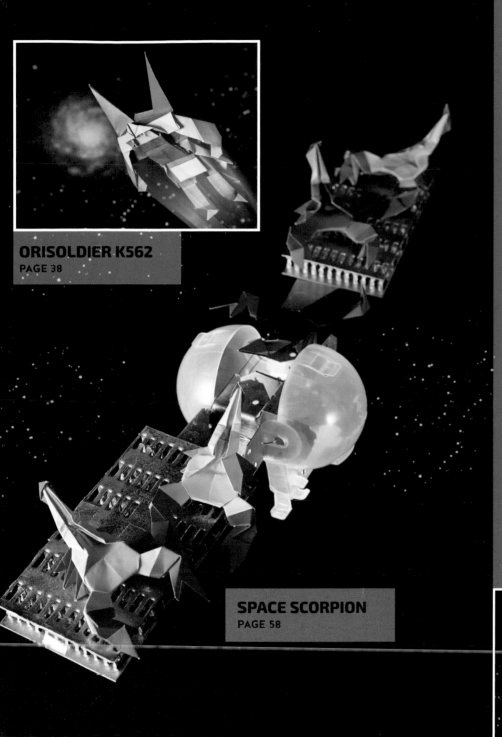

ORISOLDIER K562
PAGE 38

SPACE SCORPION
PAGE 58

DATE: 2255.04.08

REPORT: A new threat appears in space. It is believed that when mankind defeated SHRED, DNA data and debris was spread into space and led to the spontaneous creation of new enemies, called SPACE SCORPIONS. They paralyze satellite functions by attaching and injecting viruses. The SPACE SCORPIONS absorb energy from the satellites and their population rapidly increases. This leads to paralyzed communication and transportation systems. Humans immediately send the ORISOLDIERS to destroy the SPACE SCORPIONS. Who will be victorious?

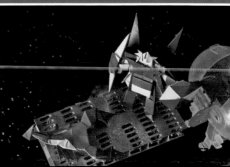

SPACE SCORPION

SHOWN ON PAGE 57

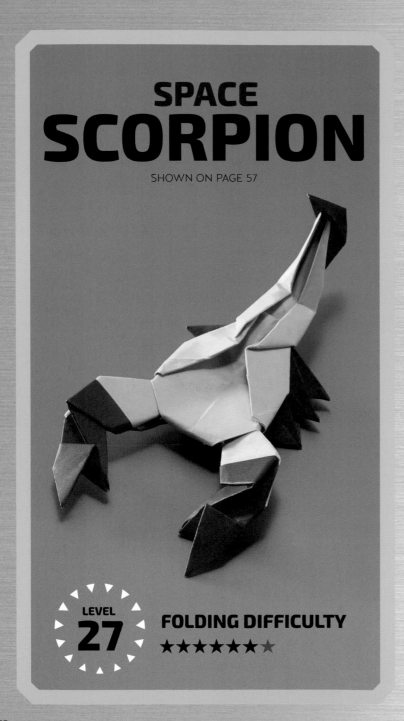

This scorpion-shaped robot has the ability to cut through iron and steel and can paralyze computers with its poisonous tail.

LEVEL 27

FOLDING DIFFICULTY
★★★★★★☆

MACHINE DATA	
TYPE	DESTROYER
POWER	★★★★★
SPEED	★★★★★
OFFENSIVE POWER	★★★★★★
DEFENSIVE POWER	★★★★★
FEATURES	» SCISSORS CRUSH » POISONOUS TAIL
ABILITY TO FLY	X

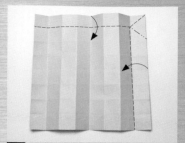

1 Make starting shape A, as shown on page 10. Fold along the outermost creases while pinching one corner in half, flattening to the right.

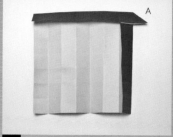

2 Completed view of step 1. Note the position of corner A.

Turn over

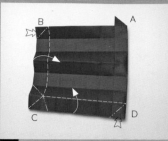

3 Fold along the outermost creases while squash folding at B and D and pinching corner C in half, flattening to the left.

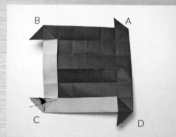

4 Fold edge to crease and unfold. Focus on corner C.

Zoom in

Rotate

5 Outside reverse fold along existing creases.

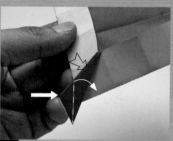

6 Open the layers and flatten as with a squash fold.

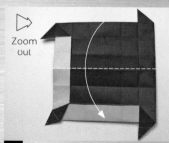

Zoom out

7 Valley fold edge to edge.

Zoom in

8 Valley fold the left corner and mountain fold the right corner to the center.

9 Open the layers symmetrically and squash fold as shown.

10 Fold the edge to the center and unfold.

11 Fold the edge to the center and unfold.

12 Fold the corner up along existing creases.

13 Bring the edges to the center and open the top flap out as shown.

 Zoom out

14 Completed view of step 13.

Turn over

15 Flatten the top flap down.

16 Fold the corner back out as shown.

Zoom in

17 Valley fold edge to edge.

18 Valley fold edge to edge.

19 Tuck the front flap inside.

▷ Zoom out

20 Fold the edges to the center and unfold.

21 Fold the corner up along existing creases.

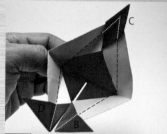

22 Keep B, C, and D folded while bringing the edges to the center.

23 Fold the flap back down. Repeat behind.

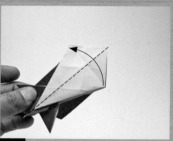

24 Fold one layer to the left.

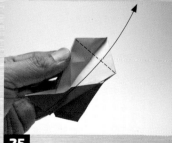

25 Fold the flap up as shown.

26 Fold one layer back to the right.

27 Repeat steps 24–26 on the left side.

28 Valley fold the sides out diagonally as shown.

29 Mountain fold the corner behind.

30 Inside reverse fold the corner inward.

Zoom in

31 Valley fold corner to corner.

32 Valley fold the corner out to form a pincer.

33 Mountain fold a corner behind.

34 Repeat steps 30–33 on the left side.

Zoom out

35 Completed view of step 34.

Turn over

Rotate

36 Valley fold the edges toward center as shown.

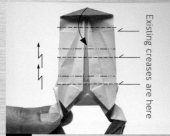

Existing creases are here

37 Pleat twice and valley fold the top down.

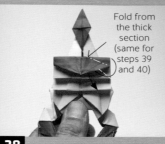

Fold from the thick section (same for steps 39 and 40)

38 Inside reverse fold as shown.

Zoom in

39 Inside reverse fold in the same way as step 38.

40 Inside reverse fold in the same way as step 38.

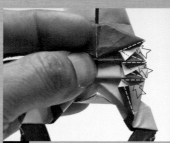

41 Open and pleat upward to squash fold. Repeat this process twice more.

42 Repeat steps 38–41 on the left side.

Zoom out

43 Pleat to cover the layers in front.

44 Completed view of step 43.

Turn over

Zoom out

45 Valley fold diagonally as shown. Note: The top of the model will also start to fold during this process. Refer to step 46 for details on finishing this area.

46 Valley fold the edge of the stinger to the center.

47 Completed view of step 46. Repeat steps 45–46 on the left side.

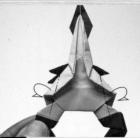

48 Mountain fold the side corners behind.

49 Pinch the end of the stinger together as shown. Valley fold the stinger forward.

SPACE SCORPION is complete!